DR YESHAYAHU (JESAIAH) BEN-AHARON — spiritual [...] d social act[...] sophical con[...] er of the Glo[...] folding, dire[...] d contributor to the Scho[...] author of *Cognitive Yoga*, *Spiri[...] in the 21st Century*, *The Spiritual Event of the Twentieth Century*, *The New Experience of the Supersensible*, *America's Global Responsibility* and *The Event in Science, History, Philosophy & Art*.

COGNITIVE YOGA: HOW A BOOK IS BORN

Heavenly Jerusalem and the Mysteries of the Human Body

Yeshayahu (Jesaiah) Ben-Aharon

TEMPLE LODGE

Temple Lodge Publishing Ltd.
Hillside House, The Square
Forest Row, RH18 5ES

www.templelodge.com

First published by Temple Lodge Publishing, 2017

© Yeshayahu Ben-Aharon 2017

The Publishers are grateful to Scott Hicks for his editorial work on the text

This book is copyright under the Berne Convention. All rights reserved. Apart from any fair dealing for the purpose of private study, research, criticism or review, no part of this publication may be reproduced, stored in a retrieval system, or transmitted in any form or by any means, electronic, electrical, chemical, mechanical, optical, photocopying, recording or otherwise, without the prior written permission of the copyright owner. Inquiries should be addressed to the Publishers

The right of Yeshayahu Ben-Aharon to be identified as the author of this work has been asserted in accordance with sections 77 and 78 of the Copyright, Designs and Patents Act, 1988

A CIP catalogue record for this book is available from the British Library

ISBN 978 1 912230 11 2

Cover by Morgan Creative
Typeset by DP Photosetting, Neath, West Glamorgan
Printed and bound by 4Edge Ltd., Essex

The paths of gods and men must merge in our time. Michael will be the great mediator between the paths of gods and the paths of human beings. Let us pay heed to his work! Then shall we be permitted to look to the future not merely with well-meaning enthusiasm but with courageous enthusiasm, then shall we find our will conjoined more and more with the divine will that has guided humanity from the beginning, then shall we feel our freedom join forces with the freedom of the gods. This is what we must feel. If we do, we shall be permitted to say each day when we have finished our daily work, hoping not for smaller but for greater things for the following day: Perhaps the gods are looking down upon us and saying: Yea, so be it.

Rudolf Steiner, lecture from 22nd September 1924, GA 346

Contents

Foreword	1
Introduction	4
1. Four Stages of Development	10
2. The Mystery of Conception	15
3. An Insurmountable Problem	22
4. Some Soul Experiences on the Threshold	34
5. A Co-Creative Journey	39
6. The Author is Pregnant	56
7. A Book is Born	62

Foreword

This little book relates some experiences I had during the spiritual research which was eventually published in my book, *Cognitive Yoga – Making Yourself a New Etheric Body and Individuality* (2016). Usually in my books and lectures I am concerned with communicating the objective results of my research and not what I experienced while doing it. But also, an objective description of what the individual soul undergoes during spiritual research can be valuable to the general study of anthroposophy and to those who pursue the spiritual path themselves. Anthroposophical spiritual schooling, if practised seriously over many years, gradually transforms all aspects of our soul life. The soul begins to experience a new life, which takes its course in previously unknown spiritual experiences and worlds. It also feels the need to understand itself ever more deeply, and from ever new points of view in this new existence. In this way, spiritual science becomes something different than its known physical expressions on the earth. First it becomes an intimate friend in the realms of soul and spirit, then it becomes a living spiritual being accompanying us, and finally, it grows to become an extended spiritual community composed of many varied beings. One gradually learns the inner language to converse and co-create with them, and receives in return cognitive and moral support. And the human soul develops a growing trust and confidence in this new companionship and community, because it feels itself ever more grounded in its own innermost independent being and becoming.

In the beginning of the twentieth century, Rudolf Steiner

founded and pioneered for humanity a fully modern path of spiritual development and research. This path is grounded in detailed and practical, individual spiritual and moral self-actualization. Being a fully modern path, it can and must be actualized freely by each person, and individualized in accord with his and her specific life conditions, capacities, and karma. Walking in this path and implementing its methods, one enters consciously into the spiritual worlds. In the spiritual worlds, one may also find the way to the spiritual being of his teacher, provided one already experienced it through one's own spiritual efforts during earthly life. If he brings this independently achieved earthly spiritual recognition with him to the spiritual worlds, he may be gracefully granted also the conscious spiritual apprenticeship in his spiritual school and community. This spiritual school, grounded in the spiritual world nearest to the earth, is an operative, active and creatively engaged community, in which the archetypal spiritual goals and plans are worked out, and constantly updated, in relation to the immediate, near, and far evolutionary possibilities afforded by human beings in the age of human freedom. The intimate soul experiences described below took place during such a co-creative consultation and instruction in this school, in a time when my spiritual research was ripe for energetic assistance and enhancement related to a specific task and problem.

These experiences reached a certain culmination during the holy days and nights of 2012, which was for me an especially rich and productive year. They took place 'behind the scenes' in my ongoing spiritual scientific investigation and practice of Cognitive Yoga, when I was confronted with a major obstacle and problem on the path of research. After struggling alone, so to speak (one is never alone in spiritual life and work), for several years, with this spiritual roadblock, I felt that I could not progress any further without consulting my spiritual teacher and colleagues. Such a consultation is a special, indeed, a festive occasion, and one must be sure in one's heart that the cause and timing is truly appropriate. Sometimes while our daily relations go on as usual with their manifold meetings, interests, and work, we feel the need for a special gathering to celebrate a holiday, create something new together, or commemorate a special person or historical event. This happens also in our spiritual life. And so it was during 2012. I felt that the time was ripe and that it would be proper and productive to prepare and wait for such a festive meeting with my spiritual colleagues. I want to share some aspects of what I experienced during this event, in the more personal and imaginative language of storytelling. It is a kind of new, individual, Christmas nativity tale, about the earthly ripening of a research problem, its heavenly conception, embryonic life, and finally the birth on earth of what becomes a physical book, printed black on white. The tale is what follows.

Introduction

'The Word becoming flesh is the first Michael revelation; the flesh becoming Spirit must be the second Michael revelation.'

Rudolf Steiner (GA 194, 22 November 1919)

Before I begin the tale, let me give some necessary background. In Chapter 4 of my book *The New Experience of the Supersensible*, I describe three main aspects of the meeting with the being of the living, resurrected Christ (the Higher Self of humanity). In this meeting, Christ stands by you to encourage you to awaken yourself to new life as a whole human being, in spirit, soul and body. It can also be said, that he gracefully offers you a unique gift, made of three potent golden seeds that you can plant in your spirit, soul and body, which—this depends of course on your own free creative spiritual activity—you may develop further independently. This is what I tried to accomplish in my anthroposophical work in my 20s and 30s, and *The New Experience of the Supersensible* offered a summary of the main investigations undertaken during this process. In that book, I could describe the independent planting and cultivation of the first two golden seeds: those planted in the spirit and soul. But the cultivation of the third seed in the body proved to be much more difficult, because it was hindered by strong obstacles. This required a development of higher and deeper cognitive-moral faculties which at that time I couldn't yet fully actualize.[*]

---

[*] As described in Chapters 4 and 5 of *The New Experience of the Supersensible*, the spiritualized soul faculties that must be developed for this work are called by Rudolf Steiner the 'Imaginative Soul', which is the result of the transformation of the Consciousness Soul, the 'Inspirative Soul', the transformed Mind Soul, and the 'Intuitive Soul', the trans-

Continued on next page

To be more specific, the cognitive-moral capacities that I could develop before my 40s were not sufficient to properly cultivate the third bodily seed. But this complete cultivation is required to fulfil through spiritual scientific work the most important spiritual task of our age, which the anthroposophically grasped impulse of the etheric Christ makes possible for the first time to free human beings. The task is to learn how to apply spiritual science to individualize the Christ Impulse not only in the spirit and soul but also in the spiritual forces of the bodies. Only by means of modern anthroposophical spiritual science is it possible today to explore, discover, and activate these deeply hidden spiritual forces, slumbering in the primordial foundations of the bodies, and bring them to full imaginative consciousness.[*]

In hindsight, I can say that this third, bodily aspect of the work, had to wait, until I reached my eighth seven-year period, in the age of 56–63, in which—usually wholly unconsciously—the forces of Spirit Man (Atman) are activated. During these years, I could experience how I was supported by forces activated through the development of Spirit Self (in the age of 42–49) and Life Spirit (49–56). This brought about a change in my faculty of Imagination, on which I was working for decades, because it could be supported by more potent spiritual forces than before. This enabled me to grasp imaginatively—but this faculty of

---

formed Sentient Soul (29 March 1913, GA 145). It was especially the third one, the 'Intuitive Soul', that needed a longer time of gestation and cultivation.

[*] This is also the reason why, in *The New Experience of the Supersensible*, the sixth chapter: 'The Creation of the New Heaven and Earth of the Earthly-Human Sun', appears to me to be the least satisfactory, because the research of the transformation of the three bodies of the earth requires the ripening of the same faculties.

Imagination was now increasingly saturated by stronger inspirative and intuitive elements—also some aspects of the potential spiritual forces of the three bodies. As I describe in detail in *Cognitive Yoga*, I could then overcome some of the powerful obstacles found in the bodies, composed of desires, drives and instincts, and penetrate consciously deeper into them. I felt that the more this eighth seven-year period progressed, for the first time I could reach my goal, to complete— in certain limits—the development of that aspect of the modern faculty of Imagination that was given to me to individualize and spiritualize by means of spiritual science. Then I could use the forces of this Imaginative Soul, supported and enhanced by the inspirative and intuitive forces, to awaken some aspects of the pure, virgin, forces hidden in the depths of the three bodies, and unite them—through the free cognitive activity of spiritual science—with the forces of the etheric Christ. And this is what I described in my book, *Cognitive Yoga*.

According to Rudolf Steiner, what is the origin and essence of these virgin forces of the 'sleeping beauty' that lie dormant and strongly guarded and protected in our unconsciousness? To answer this question, we must turn to Rudolf Steiner's investigations, given in his lecture cycle about the gospel of St Luke in September 1909. He points out that in each human being there exists even today precious residues of the original divine forces, that remained in their pure original state, as they were formed during from the evolutionary stages of old Saturn, Sun and Moon. During these three cosmic phases of our evolution, the divinely given and developed bodies: the physical, etheric and astral, were formed in their most sublime, archetypal, divine beauty and perfection. Part of them was protected also when at the beginning of the evolution of the earth, the 'I' was added and with it the luciferic egotistical influence. But the guiding divine beings spared one part from each of these bodies, and didn't let them be spoiled entirely by the luciferic and later the ahrimanic forces. That is, this unique extract of the original, sublime cosmic human being, who consists only of these pure archetypal and heavenly Adamic forces, was protected from the intervention of Lucifer at the end of Lemuria. It was preserved as pure future potentiality until the time when the first human being could be born, in which these forces could be embodied for the first time, and incarnate physically only once. This took place in the Jesus child from the line of David's son Nathan, whose birth is described in the gospel of St Luke. This Nathanic-Jesus being became the chalice that received and embodied the cosmic Higher Self of Humanity, the Christ. Now an individual extract of the same pure virgin forces is also preserved in the wholly unconscious depth of the physical, etheric and astral bodies of each human being even today. And as Jesus, in the thirtieth year of his life, in the baptism by John in the Jordan river, received into himself the cosmic Higher Self of Humanity, and united with him these purest primordial spiritual forces, so can each human being do the same. Every human being who will complete the goal of earthly evolution must also eventually fulfil, during many repeated earthly lives, the same mission that Jesus accomplished macrocosmically for humanity and the earth as a whole. This deeply unconscious, pure spiritual essence of the human being, says Rudolf Steiner,

> ... is what is born virginally in man, which unites itself during human evolution with the Christ. But it cannot unite itself with the human being without what man can develop in himself through the Christ-principle. Only what in the present human being is childlike has still the last remnant of what the being man was before he fell under the influence of Lucifer. This

> being in us, the Christ power, must newly awaken... The Christ power must unite itself with the best forces of the childlike nature in man, because by the detour through this childlike remnant will the Christ faculty suffuse with warmth the other faculties. We should make the childlike faculties in us wise, in order through it to make the other soul faculties younger.*

When through spiritual science we consciously activate these primordial, pure spiritual forces in our individual bodies, and unite them with the presently active forces of the living Christ, something else becomes possible. The more we consciously activate these Nathanic forces in us, and the more we unite them with the presently living Christ forces, the more we can individualize also the macrocosmic forces of the Nathanic being, because these forces are the archetypal forces of our purely remaining individual spiritual-bodily forces. We are then enabled to unite the awakened and activated forces of our three bodies, with their cosmic archetype. Especially significant in this regard, is the awakening and activation of the pure Nathanic etheric forces in the etheric body, because in our time the etheric Christ activates them in us also in a natural way. Rudolf Steiner describes this process in this manner:

> The first union of the etheric body that remained behind [unsullied by the luciferic temptation] with a human being happened for the first time when the Luke Jesus was born... Just as a seed that's laid in the earth produces an ear with many kernels, so Jesus' body was the soil for Adam's etheric body, the point of passage [*Durchgangspunkt*] for multiplication, and it's these multiplied etheric bodies that are waiting for us.†

---

*GA 114, lecture of 26 September 1909.
†GA 266, Esoteric Lesson of 7 December 1909.

I tried to show the consequences of carefully working through and deepening this work in the present age of Michael in my books and lectures and recently in *Cognitive Yoga*. It is therefore a real modern, timely path of *Imitatio Christi*, that is, an individualization, on an infinitely humbler microcosmic-individual scale, of the macrocosmic deed of Jesus Christ, that constitutes in each human being 'the point of passage for multiplication', that if tended to and cultivated by true spiritual science, in the modern Michaelic way, prepares us to individualize 'these multiplied etheric bodies that are waiting for us'.[*]

This is indeed a central aspect of the anthroposophically grasped and actualized meaning of the Second Coming in its fullness, as it will be realized gradually in the next 3000 years. The reappearance of Christ in the etheric world is gradually unfolding and revealing itself in the present age and in the future ages to come, because, as He said, 'The I AM is with you always, even until the end of earthly evolution.'[†]

The research described in *The New Experience of the Supersensible* and *Cognitive Yoga*, is dedicated, therefore, among others, to the Michaelic task of the present Michaelic age, the activation of the three golden seeds, in spirit, soul and body, needed to receive and individualize the fullness of the new revelation of the Etheric Christ. And in the present book, the sequel of *Cognitive Yoga*, I wish to describe some of my experiences 'behind the scenes' during the later stages of this process.

---

[*] This means that a 'copy' of this etheric body can be implanted in the individual, consciously awakened and activated pure forces of the etheric body, aided by the forces of the presently active etheric Christ, to the extent that we succeed to etherize and spiritualize our soul forces, cognition and bodies, through the modern spiritual schooling of spiritual science.
[†] Matthew 28:20.

1. Four Stages of Development

I distinguish four main phases in the development and incarnation of a specific task of spiritual research, until it is embodied in one or several means of physical expression. These four phases are grounded in a threefold process. The first part is dominated by a markedly evolutionary drive and progression, while the second part is an involutionary process. Between the two is a purely supersensible phase.

The first phase is the youthful part of the spiritual research, motivated by the heart forces, the sense of wonder, devotion and love, that underlie the quest about the human and cosmic riddles of existence, life and consciousness. It addresses concrete human and cosmic questions, which necessitate the development of task-specific, morally based, faculties of knowledge. (We must distinguish between the general, ongoing practices, designed to create harmonious development of all the cognitive and moral soul forces, which are exercised regularly, and the development of task-specific faculties. Each riddle is a task that requires the development of new and specific cognitive forces, which, once created, must be further differentiated and specialized, in accord with the concrete research tasks at hand.) This phase is mainly evolutionary, which means that it is carried by an intentional building up of our spiritual forces and faculties, growing from below upward, transforming the soul forces to higher spiritual forces of cognition.

It is a true 'springtime' of the research project, activating and actualizing the youthful, active, creative, energetic, forces of the human soul, a phase of growth and development from below upward.

The second phase begins as a phase of intensifying crisis, in which a major problem emerges and ripens, which refuses all efforts of intentional solution for a long time. I experience this phase as the ripening of the real riddle of the research project, and a sign that I am approaching nearer to its essential core. This core is, spiritually speaking, strongly guarded by its own essential spiritual nature. As I will describe below, this is a paradoxical stage in which a problem matures, comes of age, and becomes ripe for a breakthrough and metamorphosis. When the problem matures, it doesn't depend anymore on an intentional enhancement of my cognitive forces, but rather on an opposite soul gesture. The more I am ready to let go of my personal desire to reach a solution, and the more I give the problem up, the more I begin to feel how a complementary gesture from the spiritual world reveals and offers itself as a gift. This is the process by means of which the soul becomes a real, fully conscious, spiritual soul. If this process is successfully carried through, the problem, detached from me, is joined to the spiritual world, and is taken into its creative processes. We all go through this all the time, but the supersensible transformations and resolutions of our questions and problems happen during unconscious sleep, and when we awake in the morning, perhaps after many mornings, the solution may light up in our daily consciousness. This process, after all, underlies the emergence and expression of all creative human ideas, arts, discoveries and inventions in the physical world. In the case described here, my soul was invited to join the spiritualization process of the problem, and participate consciously in the otherwise unconscious night-spiritual transformation and resolution of the problem in the higher worlds.

In the spiritual calendar of the activity of the spiritual soul, this denotes the 'summertime' of the spiritual soul. After reaching the heights of personally driven intentionality and creativity, our spiritualized human efforts are taken up by the love and light-filled, cosmic spiritual sun rays and warmth: the spiritual 'butterflies' and 'bees' of the heavenly hosts. And it is in the heights of spiritual soul summer, above in the spiritual atmosphere, that the spiritual soul unites with the world spirit and is fertilized by its fruitful seeds.

It is followed by the third phase, the 'soul autumn', which is more an 'involutive' stage of spiritual pregnancy and embryonic soul life, in which the spiritual researcher regains his spiritual activity, but now in the reversed direction than in the springtime of the research. He must learn how to turn his or her activity inward to become a 'spiritual-soul mother' of the growing and developing being of the research. He learns how to foster the research embryo and nourish it, together with its spiritual parents, who continue to nourish and support it at the same time, until it is ready for earthly expression.

The fourth phase is then the actual physical birth, the physical expression, be it through the spoken word, artistic creation, social initiative or as in our case here, in the form of a physically written book. In this 'winter season' of the research, the birth is prepared, through a series of advent events and processes, during which, especially in the soul's spiritual holy days and nights, the being of the research becomes ready to enter fully into earthly life and existence.

It must be clear that the real spiritual development, problematization, fertilization and conception, pregnancy and birth of a concrete spiritual research work in physical life, is the result of a long and complex creative process. Before a book is written down, a problem of research must mature and open to real spiritual fertilization and pure supersensible growth and transformation in the spiritual world itself. Then it goes through a process that can be compared to the process of conception, pregnancy and birth of a human being in the physical world. While on the one hand, the final written book or work of art is a personal creation, whose coming into being is naturally nourished and shaped by the thoughts, feelings and experiences of our individual human soul, on the other hand, it is also an independent spiritual being that has a life of its own. And this continuous creative interaction and interrelationship between the human soul and spirit and the spiritual worlds, is the living essence of this whole life cycle of creation and creativity.

Spiritual research, therefore, from beginning to end, is for me a sacred mystery process; a scientific, artistic and dramatic experience, an individualized Christmas nativity tale. In spiritual research, the investigator is fully aware of the fact that he co-creates in a project that has many parents. On the one hand, he knows himself to be mother, father and child of this process, while on the other he is fully aware that many other beings feel the same, and he is deeply grateful for their graceful co-parenting. He knows that the new being is a real, actual, living, co-production, the result of a mutual and multiple fertilization and inspiration, conception, pregnancy and birth, between him and the beings of the spiritual world. It's a wholly new, creative and lively community creation, a new art of spiritual procreation and propagation, taking place between earth and heaven, humanity and the gods; a preparation and example of wonderful future possibilities, on the path of evolving humanity. He knows that this being is nourished from two sides simultaneously, and that parallel with the inner soul and spiritual experiences he undergoes during the research, the new spiritual being is carried and taken care of by his spiritual colleagues and partners. They belong together like a sacred family, and through the love and caring of the spiritual and human parents, a new being, the spiritual child, is conceived in the spiritual world and in the human soul, and then can also be born in the physical world.

2. The Mystery of Conception

Prior to its conception, incarnation and birth, the future book lives a pre-earthly spiritual life as a part of the whole soul and spiritual being of the author. At this time, the potential book is still a complex web of research problems and riddles that the text will eventually express and embody in human thoughts, words, and deeds. In this phase, it is not yet possible to distinguish its existence as an independent and separate being. The work's independent existence, relatively speaking, begins only from the moment of conception. As I described above, for fertilization and conception to occur, the problematization process of the research must be sufficiently ripe. The searching and questioning has been growing and gathering intensity in the soul and spiritual-activity of the spiritual scientist, until the spiritual core of the research, its main riddle, becomes problematic enough to ripen into a complete impasse. As this phase makes up the crucial central stage of transition from the physical cognitive process to the spiritual one, I would like to explain it again.

Though it may appear as a paradox to our ordinary understanding, this 'ripeness' does not denote the phase of final completeness. This ripeness is a final stage of the human spiritualized cognitive process. But from a spiritual point of view it is also the beginning of a new phase. The ripening process of a problem includes everything that leads to the blossoming of the main riddle that causes and motivates the research in the first place. During the problematization phase, the research process temporarily comes to a halt. This happens after the whole process is gathered together in intensified contraction and concentration like the bud of a flower. The real 'blossoming' will then take place when the researcher gives the problem up, and lets it open and subsequently unite with the spiritual world. I know that my work is ripe precisely when I arrive at an impasse on a threshold; at a problem that I cannot solve using all my previously self-acquired cognitive forces. This seems like a paradox from the ordinary point of view that can only think in a linear fashion and that believes that all problems have straightforward linear solutions. But spiritually speaking, one can only reach a certain intensity of self-enhanced cognitive activity, and as the wakeful active day must give place to the unconscious sleep at night, so does the research process, only it does so in a fully conscious way. The fruits of its most intensive creative, human activity, must also be surrendered and offered as a gift to the higher worlds. Of course, before this major impasse is reached, I experience many smaller and bigger ones during the many turns and meanderings that always characterize a complex research project. Such obstacles are eventually resolved by means of the gradual enhancement of my spiritual faculties, through the whole training and the meditative exercises used in the research of this specific domain. Therefore, I distinguish a major crisis from a lesser one, by its persistent impenetrability and consistent refusal to give in to the most intense voluntary, intentional, cognitive efforts, during a much longer period. Only then is the problem truly 'ripe', spiritually speaking, and in this sense, it opens like a flower to the higher worlds, and can be fertilized by a specific and concrete, if often very subtle, indication, hint and impulse.

What is the soul and spirit process that leads one to the stage of such ripe, exhaustive, helplessness? In our common language, these terms denote weakness, but to the spiritual scientist the opposite is the case. (We must become accustomed to the fact that the meanings of terms that we use in our physical life are reversed when we enter spiritual life.) With time, one learns the art of problematizing: how to foster and nourish an unsolvable problem. Only after many efforts and struggles can one truly know that one is on the verge of a real metamorphosis, a veritable breakthrough, having accomplished everything that one can do thus far. One must now 'go to sleep', so to speak—only in full consciousness—and develop the soul mood of peaceful release, devoted listening, and grateful acceptance of whatever the true fate of the work would turn out to be.

As we shall see in detail in Chapter 3 below, when the problem is ripe, growing out of a prolonged time of productive spiritual research, the soul develops a special mood that can be described as active, courageous resignation. We give up the self-willed desire to achieve progress and success. This mood of creative resignation and surrender, when we let go of our personal control of the research process, frees the riddle from our intentional grip, ideas and representations, and therefore it can begin to reveal to us its true essence in the spiritual worlds. Such ripened research is always accepted by the beings that guide and support human evolution in our age. They are Michaelic beings, characterized by the fact that they accept only the creative, fully individualized, human work accomplished by means of free and conscious spiritual activity on the earth. Michael, says Rudolf Steiner, doesn't influence the human will; he expects humans to develop their spiritual work in full freedom:

> We carry up into a spiritual world the knowledge of Nature here attained, or again, the creations of naturalistic art, or the religious sentiments working naturalistically in the soul... And as we carry all this upward—if we develop the necessary faculties—we do indeed encounter Michael ... Michael is a

being who reveals nothing if we do not bring him something from our diligent spiritual work on Earth... Michael will be the true spiritual hero of Freedom; he lets men do, and he then takes what becomes of human deeds, receives it and carries it on and out into the cosmos, to continue in the cosmos what men themselves cannot yet do with it... But when man does things out of spiritual activity or inner freedom, then Michael carries the human earthly deed out into the cosmos; so that it becomes cosmic deed.[*]

And this applies of course also to Rudolf Steiner, the leader of Michael's stream on earth and the 'headmaster' of the human department in his cosmic school. Once human beings have sown, grown, and rightly cultivated a creative, spiritualized and truthful fruit in their human garden, Michael and his partners affirmatively accept it, develop it further in the spiritual world, and invite us to participate in its continuous spiritual development. We must bear this in mind when I describe below the spiritual side of the event of cooperative spiritual fertilization and conception, since this is an attempt to describe such a creative mutual interaction between a human being and the Michaelic school in the spiritual worlds, because, indeed, 'The paths of gods and men must merge in our time. Michael will be the great mediator between the paths of gods and the paths of human beings. Let us pay heed to his work!... Then shall we feel our freedom join forces with the freedom of the gods.'[†]

Now, the following fact must be emphasized: fertilization and conception take place only if the spiritual world offers them freely as a loving act of grace. The ripe problem must fully release itself from the soul and be transformed into an

---
[*] Lecture from 13 January 1924, GA 233a.
[†] Lecture from 22 September 1924, GA 346.

independent spiritual being that opens and offers itself in loving surrender to the higher worlds and beings. Then, like a flower opening to the sun's rays, it can be fertilized by the higher worlds 'without sin', that is, without being coloured any further by my soul's personal desires, wishes and expectations. In this way, the problem signals that it is ready for a sacred meeting and consultation with the teachers and colleagues of the Michaelic school through which the holy spirit—the divine macrocosmic spirit—works. The meeting with these colleagues can therefore be compared to a virginal conception. One can receive truly new impulses purely from the higher worlds. This is experienced as a serious, sacred and festive marriage, a mutual, reciprocal, giving and receiving between humanity and the spiritual worlds, earth and heaven. The marriage is followed by spiritual fertilization and conception, taking place wholly in the supersensible world, between the human soul and the spiritual world.

That is, the fertilization and moment of conception takes place when the ripened problem, developing in the human soul, opens and discharges its spiritualized essence, sending it upward to the spiritual world. We know that it is accepted when we experience that a spark of creative impulse lights up, rapidly conciliating between the spiritual world and the expanding and self-surrendering spiritual soul. To begin with, the origin of this spark is shrouded in mystery because it is not immediately clear where it is coming from, and the spiritual search for its origin finds it neither in the soul nor in the spiritual worlds. On further investigation, it turns out that the spark only springs forth when the human soul and the spiritual world have come to a specific, determined, proximity to each other. This proximity creates a positive tension that leads to the event of fertilization and conception. When this proximity has been reached, and we can zoom in closer to observe it, we see that what appears from afar as one spark is really a multicoloured, multifaceted messenger being, which is made of a composition of many sparks that cohere together but do not mesh entirely; they retain their multiplicity despite their intimate composition. First, I could observe that there were actually two sparks that were flashing back and forth from one pole to the other, from the spirit pole to the soul pole and from the soul to the spirit, simultaneously. They merged together in such a way that they reciprocally exchanged a soul potency and spirit impulse with each other, and it is this exchange—that doesn't extinguish the singular being of each but rather enhances it—which appears as one radiant and multicoloured being, a composite spark. Furthermore, at the same time, many other sparks are flashing to and fro, like shooting stars, through the whole cosmic periphery, illuminating the spirit firmament with magnificent fireworks. As they merge their forces together they become part of the composition of the spark, welding their cosmic seeds into the event of conception. You can also say, metaphorically speaking, that they congratulate the spirit bridegroom and soul bride on their coming together and they consecrate the moment of their union. They paint and compose a starry canopy and aura enveloping and sheltering the soul of the spiritual investigator and the beings of the spiritual world, as they interpenetrate and mutually fertilize each other, celebrating this event of graceful destiny.

On further imaginative investigation, we discover that the composite spark is the external appearance of a real spiritual being, a messenger of the gods, that flies to and fro between the soul, that becomes increasingly spirit-like, and the spiritual world, that receives it; the spiritual world then envelops the fruits and seeds offered by the human soul and takes them lovingly to its own spiritual heart. The active, radiant, messenger, guides, on the one hand, the self-surrendering soul upwards, and on the other, directs towards it the related spiritual impulse. He brings together the spiritual-soul bride and the spiritual bridegroom under a common hallowed aura.

From the moment of conception on, this seed continues its development in the human soul, nourished through the interactions between the human soul and the spiritual worlds. After this event, I enter a phase of soul-spiritual embryonic development, which, unlike human pregnancy, has no fixed duration. The duration of the spiritual pregnancy is individually adapted for each field and task of supersensible research and spiritual creation. In some cases, it can be also rather long.*

---

*For example, the complex research that underlies my book, *The New Experience of the Supersensible*, started at the end of the 1970s. It was then problematized and conceived in the middle of the '80s and was physically written, that is, born, as late as 1989–90, and then was published in 1995.

3. An Insurmountable Problem

As mentioned above, at critical stages of the development of my spiritual research, a more conscious cooperation is called for between the researcher and the spiritual beings that guide and protect the work-in-progress in the spiritual worlds. The experience I am going to report below took place after many years, during which my research confronted a major problem. Let me now explain what this problem was, and then describe how it was used as a subject of instruction by my spiritual colleagues.

As I pointed out in the Introduction above, the goal of the research concerning *Cognitive Yoga* was to deepen my original research, first presented in my book, *The New Experience of the Supersensible*, published in 1995. At that time, I couldn't advance further in the needed direction, which was—as I pointed out above in the Introduction—to develop the Michaelic Yoga method created by Rudolf Steiner, to individualize Christ's gifts, and use them to penetrate to the deeper and pure spiritual forces of the bodies. I knew from experience that if I did my work, help would be given from the Michaelic school, and that Michael's power seeks to penetrate and spiritualize not only our soul forces, but also through them, the material world and the physical body.

Steiner described it thus:

> Now the Michaelic Intelligence is on the earth, it strikes far deeper, it strikes down even into the earthly element of man... Thus, that which is influenced by Michael will appear as an immediate, physically creative, physically formative power.[*]

---
[*] Lecture from 3 August 1924, GA 237.

An Insurmountable Problem 23

Searching for these matter and body spiritualizing forces of Michael, I had to develop ever new and ever stronger cognitive forces. I have experienced this spiritualizing power of Michael's redeemed intelligence in each cognitive activity I developed through *The Philosophy of Freedom*, and this served me as a guiding line of force in all my work, from the very beginning. I knew therefore where to search for IT and how to experience IT (the liberated Michaelic intelligence), when IT weaves and streams as you actualize its forces. I therefore also knew that the more I actualized them, the more they would lead me to find the way and access to the deep, unconscious, virgin 'Nathanic forces' that lie dormant and strongly guarded in the spiritual depth of our physical, etheric and astral bodies. But we can accomplish this only to the extent that the spiritualized cognitive forces can transform these more firmly consolidated bodily forces and elements. And this requires, naturally, a deepening and strengthening of the active, conscious *moral* forces of your whole, embodied, human being. I couldn't do this yet when I was working on the research published in my first books, but I nevertheless continued patiently to develop my forces in this direction. During my 40s and 50s—alongside other research projects—I was also constantly working on this development, but repeatedly came to a standstill in the same astral-bodily point.

To confront this central problem, I augmented, differentiated and specified my general continuous work with the basic anthroposophical instructions for meditation given in Rudolf Steiner's fundamental books, *Knowledge of the Higher Worlds* and *Occult Science*, with the indications given in the lecture cycle *The Boundaries of Natural Science*. In these lectures, he outlines the new soul and spiritual breathing process, which he compares to the ancient yoga practice. This practice aims, first, to separate thinking and sense perception from each other; second, to spiritualize and exhale thinking out to the spiritual world, and inhale the spiritualized stream of sense perception into the bodies. This causes pure thinking, eventually, to be transformed into spiritual Inspiration, and pure sense perception, streaming into the bodies, to be transformed into the faculty of Imagination. Finally, in a higher synthesis, both are recombined to create the highest faculty of Intuition. The general backbone of the whole yoga process is the constant purification, spiritualization and exhalation of thinking by means of *The Philosophy of Freedom*, and the specific path of developing the faculty of Imagination—which was my main task—is concentrated on the etherization of sense perceptions and their inhalation into the bodies. While thinking is continuously spiritualized outside the body, the research in the field of sense perception aims to spiritualize and extract intensive life forces from ordinary sense perceptions and inhale them directly into the body, bypassing any ordinary thinking and representation.

During the years, facing as I did the impenetrability of the bodies, I felt the need to start afresh my cognitive work in this domain, on several occasions. The same need, to start afresh, was felt again most intensively towards the end of my 50s. Though I had been developing the spiritual cognitive faculties of spiritualized thinking and perception for several decades, and had used them in previous research tasks, for the present task I needed to start again afresh, only from my present ordinary daily consciousness, and progress from the ground up, step by step, without using my previously developed cognitive forces.[*] When I did this, I could feel a significant

---

[*] This practice of erasing previous achievements and starting afresh from the beginning is a precondition for true progress in any real, empirical, spiritual scientific work. It is what makes you younger and younger, spiritually speaking, the older you become physically.

difference between my previous and the presently developing capacities. From my early 20s, activating and spiritualizing pure thinking, was easier for me, and with its help I could also carry my sense perceptions outside the body and spiritualize them out there. But the task that Rudolf Steiner gave in his above-mentioned lectures, to purify sense perceptions and inhale them consciously into the body, proved to be much more difficult. With the help of spiritualized thinking I could purify and extract the etheric forces from sense perception, but when I tried to inhale them into the deeper levels of bodies, I reached the above-mentioned obstacle and impasse.

Now I started to apply this method again. Basically speaking, my practice had two main stages: first, I worked to develop and enhance the cognitive faculties of pure thinking and sense perception necessary for the task. Second, I tried again to exercise the inhalation process of the extracted etheric forces of sense perception. While doing so, I trained myself to carefully observe the following three elements:

a) How the bodies are stimulated by the fructifying inhalation of these forces in the various parts of the bodies.
b) How the bodies interact with them.
c) How the bodies co-create new life forces with them.

This time I could indeed notice that I was making some progress in this work in comparison to previous years. I could now inhale these forces more fully into the higher parts of the brain, which was not possible before to such an extent. However, regarding the inhalation of the forces extracted from sense perception into the lower and deeper parts of the brain—and their connection with the middle and especially lower parts of the body—the problem was again becoming increasingly difficult. Eventually it became clear to me that with my best present cognitive faculties I couldn't breathe in and assimilate the extracted forces beyond a given and seemingly impassable, bodily barrier and threshold. This was the case especially when I was trying to delve through the solar plexus and related bodily parts, organs and processes, and their correlated astral forces. These proved to be too dense and stubborn, hard and impenetrable, and could not be fructified by the etheric forces in the desired manner. I became aware that I couldn't produce sufficiently robust life forces out of my spiritual activity that would enable me to accomplish this task.

This task, in other words, meant (pictorially speaking) to create the necessary key and password to cross this threshold and descend into these lower bodily forces, processes and organs. I could acutely experience that the cause of this problem is to be found in deeply ingrained bodily-soul forces, of luciferic-ahrimanic origins. Eventually, I concluded that once more I would have to give up the possibility of continuing this research to its desired completion. And then, when I truly 'gave my problem up' I began to feel the above-mentioned inner prompting that indicated that I might prepare myself to engage more consciously with the 'other side', with my colleagues, and that some indications were given that a unique advent was underway.

This preparation, mind you, amounts to this, that the above-described impenetrable problem became a real-life problem and concern of my whole being, in spirit, soul, and body. That is, I experienced it for many years in my whole being, until it became ripe enough to be given up and carried through the portal of the spiritual world. You must become the problem, consciously, because you *are* the problem, of course, all the time. The 'problem' is nothing less than your entire human constitution, incarnated in bodies hardened by the luciferic-ahrimanic instincts, drives, inclinations and habits, influencing us from early childhood so powerfully, especially in the present age.

When I encountered this unsolvable problem again, as part of my renewed research, I was redirected to Rudolf Steiner's reports about his own struggles in this domain. I was of course aware of these reports for many years, but was occupied with research problems in other domains of spiritual scientific work. I felt a need to contemplate again, but now from a different point of view, Rudolf Steiner's descriptions of his struggles in creating a truly modern spiritual science, Anthroposophy, based on a fully spiritual understanding of the bodily nature of the human being as part of his threefold being. I therefore returned to Rudolf Steiner's explanations of the reasons why he didn't complete and publish his only unfinished book, a big part of which was written down in the year 1910.* In this book, Rudolf Steiner says, he intended to give a first characterization of the physical human being as a being of the 12 senses, as part of a new study of the constitution of the human being, in body, soul and spirit, which would create a new foundation for Anthroposophy, as a modern science of the spirit.

Many years later, he describes in an exceptionally personal way, the obstacles he encountered in this field. He only mentions it in the first two lecture cycles given as the founding of the High School for Spiritual Science in 1920 and 1921. The first reference is in the sixth lecture of *The Boundaries of Natural Science* (GA 322), where he first introduced the new method of Michaelic or Cognitive Yoga on which my work is based. And the next year he referred to it, for a second and final time, in the sixth lecture in the second High School lec-

---

*It remained incomplete and was published posthumously with the title: *Anthroposophy, A Fragment*, GA 45.

ture cycle, *Anthroposophy and Science (Observation of Nature, Experimentation, Mathematics, and the Stages of Spiritual Scientific Research)*, given on 22 March 1921 in Stuttgart (GA 324).

In the first reference, in the lecture from 2 October 1920, he says:

> If one desires to do real research concerning human physiology, thinking must be excluded and the picture-forming activity of the senses sent inward, so that the physical organism reacts by creating Imaginations. This is a path that is only just beginning in the development of Western culture, but it is the path that must be trodden if the influence that streams over from the East, and would lead to decadence if it alone were to prevail, is to be confronted with something capable of opposing it, so that our civilization may take a path of ascent and not of decline. Generally speaking, however, it can be said that human language itself is not yet sufficiently developed to be able to give full expression to the experiences that one undergoes in the inner recesses of the soul. And it is at this point that I would like to relate a personal experience to you.
>
> Many years ago, in a different context, I tried to give expression to what might be called a science of the human senses. In spoken lectures, I succeeded to some extent in putting this science of the twelve senses into words, because in speaking it is more possible to turn language this way and that and ensure understanding by means of repetitions, so that the deficiencies of our language, which is not yet capable of expressing these supersensible things, is not so strongly felt. Strangely enough, however, when I wanted many years ago to write down what I had given as actual anthroposophy and to put it into a form suitable for a book, the outer experiences, on being interiorized, became so sensitive that language simply failed to provide the words; and I believe that the beginning of the text — several sheets of print — lay for some five or six years at the printer's. It was because I wanted to write the whole book

in the style in which it began that I could not continue writing, for the simple reason that at the stage of development I had then reached, language refused to furnish the means for what I wished to achieve. Afterward I became overloaded with work, and I still have not been able to finish the book. Anyone who is less conscientious about what he communicates to his fellow men out of the spiritual world might perhaps smile at the idea of being held up in this way by a temporarily insurmountable difficulty. But whoever really experiences and can permeate with a full sense of responsibility what occurs when one attempts to describe the path that Western humanity must follow to attain Imagination knows that to find the right words entails a great deal of effort. As a meditative schooling, it is relatively easy to describe, and this has been done in my book, *Knowledge of the Higher Worlds and Its Attainment*. If one's aim, however, is to achieve definite results such as that of describing the essential nature of man's senses—a part, therefore, of the inner make-up and constitution of humanity—it is then that one encounters the difficulty of grasping Imaginations and presenting them in sharp contours by means of words.

Nevertheless, this is the path that Western humanity must follow. And just as the man of the East could experience through his mantras the entry into the spiritual nature of the external world, so must the Westerner, leaving aside the entire psychology of association, learn to enter into his own being by attaining the realm of Imagination. Only by penetrating the realm of Imagination will he acquire the true knowledge of humanity that is necessary for humanity to progress. (2 October 1920, GA 322)

In the second reference, given in the lecture from 22 March 1921, Rudolf Steiner speaks more explicitly about the inward cause of this difficulty:

It became increasingly clear to me that before one could finish the book called *Anthroposophy*, in the form intended at

> that time, one must have certain experiences of inner vision... One must first be able to take what one perceives as soul-spiritual activity working in the nervous system and carry it further inward, until one comes to the point where one sees the entire soul-spiritual activity—which one grasps in Imagination and Inspiration—crossing itself. This crossing point is really a line, in a vertical direction if looked at schematically... One goes consciously into oneself, but again and again one is thrown back, and instead of what I would call an inner view, one gets something not right. One must overcome the inward counterblow that develops. (22 March 1921, GA 324)

For me, in the place in which I was stuck for such a long time, this last sentence constituted an important, indeed, crucial confirmation of my experience: 'One must overcome the inward counterblow that develops.' And this helped me to find the right way to comprehend and grasp my problem, because I could connect the experience of this counterblow or being thrown or pushed back, with the central problem of the *Cognitive Yoga* research, that Rudolf Steiner described in this manner:

> The experiences of the senses of smell, taste and touch are sedimented as it were on top of what we would have experienced through the senses of balance, movement and life ... through the fact that they are imposed on one another, there arises a solid self-consciousness in man; thereby he feels himself as a real self.[*]

I could also experience how the sense of smell, in addition to the effect it has on the bodily senses of life, movement and balance, powerfully influences the higher

---

[*] GA 322, lecture of 3 October 1920, and see also GA 326, lecture of 1 January 1923.

cognitive faculties. It has therefore (together with the senses of taste and touch) a central position, in creating the sedimented, hard, unsurpassable threshold below the middle of the body. I could very clearly experience the fact that our modern, intellectual, analytic thinking, is strongly bound to this sense, and what is more, that this hardened intellect is a direct metamorphosis of the sense of smell.* I therefore took it as my second major point of entry to the spiritualization of the senses and the lower body. Now because in the spiritualization of smell, together with taste and touch, one confronts and spiritualizes the instinctive activity of this analytic, brain-bound intellect of modern humanity, one creates also a powerful and trustworthy spiritual sword. We need this sword to support the spiritualization of the fallen cosmic intelligence, which is Michael's primary concern in our age; and one must confront the ahrimanic, *instinctual* side of the intellect if one would find the way, armed by the etheric Christ impulse, to the virgin, pure Adamic forces in the unconscious depth of the body.†

As was said above, I wish to use this problem, which I researched and described in my book *Cognitive Yoga*, as an example of the mutual connection between the spiritual researcher working on the earth and his spiritual teacher in the spiritual worlds. And while I had been doing my spiritual research for some decades now (my interest in the task of Michaelic Yoga started from the very beginning of my anthroposophical work), I couldn't but become conscious of the fact that my teacher took special interest in the progress of this problem. I could feel a certain intensification of his

---

*GA 180, lecture of 26 December 1917.
†I have described this process in detail in Chapter 5, 'The Knowledge Drama of the Second Coming', in my book: *The New Experience of the Supersensible*.

attention and the prompting from the spiritual world was becoming more noticeable, as I reached again—now for a major second time—this specific major obstacle.*

---

*To prevent misunderstandings, it must be said that Rudolf Steiner's work took place on an infinitely higher cognitive supersensible level than my own, with fully developed imaginative, inspirative and intuitive supersensible faculties, while I am working on developing *some aspects* of the imaginative faculty alone. (Naturally, the same problem can be studied on different levels of spiritual cognition by means of different cognitive faculties, and yet it is the same problem, and this is also the case in the above-mentioned bodily problem.) However, in this connection, the following must also be considered, otherwise it may *appear* that in my book, *Cognitive Yoga*, for example, I describe etheric processes that belong to higher stages of cognition than Imagination. Such a seeming contradiction is resolved, if we take *fully* into account the consequence of the fact that, in our time, as Rudolf Steiner points out, the modern 'Damascus Experience' will become, for the first time in human evolution, *a naturally given initiation*. Those human beings who undergo this initiation, he says, 'will not require documentary evidence in order to recognize Christ, but they will have direct knowledge as is today possessed only by the initiates', and 'all the faculties that today can be acquired only by means of initiation will in the future be universal faculties of humanity. This condition of soul, this experiencing of soul, is called in esotericism the "Second Coming of Christ".' (GA 118, 18 April 1910.) Another aspect of this unique development is that it will cause 'the force of Imagination to flow into the general intellectual consciousness of humanity', and the forces of the Christ Impulse (now operating in the etheric world), 'will imprint these human Imaginations into the cosmos', endowing them with real spiritual substance. (The Freedom of Man and the Age of Michael, 22. 2. 1925, GA 26.) This gives the Imaginations the saturation with real inspirative and intuitive *elements*, that must, however, be clearly distinguished from the fully developed faculties of Inspiration and Intuition. Such subtle distinctions and differentiations must be made if we wish to communicate results of

(Footnote continued on next page)

real spiritual scientific research. This can only be done if we formulate and shape our concepts with exact contours and outlines, on the one hand, while on the other enhance greatly the mobility and flexibility of our thinking, to view each phenomenon from many and diverse points of view. Let it also be borne in mind that one must be thoroughly conscientious regarding spiritual scientific research and its communication. One can certainly have, while working to develop systematically some inspired and intuited aspects that belong to the faculty of Imagination, real inspirative and intuitive *experiences*. However, one will not use the results of *these* experiences, when one wishes to communicate a fully authorized result of spiritual scientific research, which one will confine strictly to the limits of one's fully individualized spiritual faculty (the Imaginative faculty in our case here).

4. Some Soul Experiences on the Threshold

Before I offer an example of a practical cooperation with my colleagues in the spiritual worlds, it may be useful to share also some of the soul experiences that are necessary as preparation for such cooperation. This preparation is required, because one will have to cross the threshold in a certain way to accomplish it. This preparatory process is an essential intermediary stage in between the inner soul activity and the objective spiritual world, connecting both across the threshold that separates them in ordinary consciousness. Crossing the threshold isn't an intellectual or psychic affair; it necessitates a thorough transformation of the soul that also changes some parts of the three bodies in a permanent way. It must establish a singular soul mood and disposition, an inclination and habit, which brings the human soul and the spiritual world harmoniously together. Otherwise, one will have tumultuous and disharmonious experiences as one draws near the threshold, and this may affect one's mental, moral, and physical life adversely. This mood and disposition must become a robust, immanent, habit and inclination, and a deeply ingrained spiritual instinct, of the modern human soul. It alone can safeguard our human wholeness by continuously vitalizing and rejuvenating the heart life in the middle of our being and anchoring it in the etheric body. As I have shown in my books, this transformed etheric body and imaginative cognition, is the first level that constitutes the real supersensible bridge, in the middle of our whole being, between the physical and spiritual worlds.

As indicated above, when a research problem becomes imprinted deeply enough in the spirit, soul and body, and I feel a prompting and intimation from the other side, I know it signals that an occasion may be approaching in which a new collaborative venture with my colleagues in the spiritual world may become possible. In such a time, I foster a special 'soul vigil' that I have developed through the years, which allows me to sustain an unobtrusive, subtle, yet heightened awareness also during my daily life and chores, to make myself available—day and night—to the advent of the moment of the event, and to do so without altering or impairing my daily duties. It is important to emphasize that the annunciation of such an advent may be a passing and unremarkable event, and it is usually not a dramatic affair, adorned with supersensible appearances and spiritual fireworks. Quite the contrary. In conscious, modern spiritual life and research, you must prove your readiness, and demonstrate your heightened awareness and self-made cognitive faculties, and the beings of the spiritual worlds approach you in such a way that will 'test' your readiness. The test amounts to this: that they will be unobtrusive and unnoticeable to ordinary consciousness. It is the strictest code of conduct kept by all the beneficial, Michaelic beings, that free, modern daily human consciousness should be never encroached upon, and therefore it will never be addressed directly by them. They will never intervene, infringe and influence human freedom even in the slightest way. Through Rudolf Steiner they gave us all the tools needed to raise ourselves to their level—to the first, etheric level, to begin with. There they can meet and address us face to face, because we have exercised and independently actualized their gifts, and have proved the force of our free devotion, truthfulness, and love. You must first grow towards them for them to approach you, that is, you are the first one to initiate this contact, and if it's truly a free and truthful initiative, it will always be answered positively. Then it will be entirely up to you to demonstrate that you can 'read the occult script',* and decipher the spiritual language in which the spiritual events and the deeds of the beings are 'written' (that is, the way they express themselves), because it is only through this language that you can communicate with them. As far as our physical life is concerned, therefore, they offer only a hint and sign that you can only perceive and interpret if you have developed the appropriate faculties yourself. Therefore, I have trained my wakeful cognition to pay subtle attention to the smallest fluctuations, ripples and undercurrents of life, weaving imperceptibly beneath the noisy commerce of ordinary soul life. Yes, indeed, those unnoticed, humble things are often the harbingers of the great spiritual revelations and discoveries!

For example, such invitations may assume the form of a hushed, unrelated, unintentional thought, that passes between the lines of our ordinary soul life, an unaccustomed feeling nuance, bodily presentiments and forebodings, a free floating daydream, and similar subtle events that flicker in between the hidden and unnoticed twilight moments of our ongoing daily soul business; or it may well be a natural occurrence, like a fleeting bird song, a passing, rustling gush of wind, or a crow that flies from east to west. Naturally, it could be almost anything, depending on your individual case. For example, a faithful old friend, the red-breasted European Robin, has often served as a welcoming and delightful spirit messenger for me. He blesses our garden with his shy yet joyful and poetic presence, coming punctually on the first day

---

*This is as part of the 'water trial', as it is called in Rudolf Steiner's book, *Knowledge of the Higher Worlds* (Chapter 3, 'Initiation').

of November, to spend the winter in the mild temperatures of Israel, and often accompanying me also when I travel to Scandinavia and Europe during the summers.

Let me emphasize again, however, that such hints are only signs, pointing to an approaching advent of the event, and there is absolutely nothing forceful about them. Exactly the opposite is the case: they are expressed and dressed up in such a way that only your awakened, alert, etherized, consciousness can experience them at all. This is a holy concern of the spiritual beings who serve Michael and Christ in our age. The luciferic and ahrimanic beings, on the other hand, are precisely noisy, intrusive, manipulative and persuasive. They want to capture your soul to serve their goals and therefore all means are justified in their eyes to achieve this.

This specific state of wakeful awareness and vigil, demands that in such moments, my feelings of devotion would sustain an inner, wakeful listening, without any specific expectation or desire. I know also that if I can listen deeply enough, and sustain the listening uninterruptedly for long enough, soon I will hear the welcoming word or tone, and when I follow its footsteps, I will be able to cross over safely and peacefully, and experience the lucid awakening of supersensible cognition, in tranquility and soul balance and harmony. Then I may safely be summoned to the other side. When such a hint has been registered and deciphered, I know that it signals that a pathway is opened from both sides whose vitality may help release, activate and unfold the wings of my soul and carry me invigorated and safe through to the spiritual world.

Such intimate soul moods, habits and experiences are the homeopathically administered sacred bread and wine, as well as the salt and water, with the necessary grounding dose of ash, of real daily spiritual life. They create (among many other conditions that cannot be described further here) the solid soul foundations, supported by what becomes with the years a certain grounding *spiritual instinct*, upon which a secure and stable bridge can be built, that alone can sustain the safe and healthy passageway from this side to the other and back. It establishes moments of a joint, synchronized rhythm, through which a mutually connected, human-world heartbeat is constituted. It is a vital and safe, healthy and stable, life-rhythm of crossing and transportation over the otherwise rather stormy and treacherous river of Lethe, the world's abyss of spirit forgetfulness and luciferic-ahrimanic labyrinths and reversals. (Goethe described his imaginative perception of this bridge in his wonderful legend, *The Green Snake and the Beautiful Lily*.)

However, this must be strictly observed: the bridge should only serve you for as long as your kind hosts decide that the event will last. The duration is not of your concern nor should you desire to control it. However, in the age of freedom, it will depend again entirely on your own truthfulness, also in our supersensible life on the other side. You alone can decipher your event's hints and signs, to know when the event's end is drawing near. Egotistic, arbitrary desires to prolong supersensible experience and to intensify our personal enjoyments and bliss beyond the limits prescribed in the 'invitation letter', would become not only counterproductive to the true goals of the research project at hand, but eventually also mentally and morally unsound. Fundamentally, rightly preparing for the invitation, and letting oneself be carried by the grace of the advent of the event, is the only guarantee for its appropriate, timely, duration, preventing it from becoming either ahrimanically condensed and shortened or luciferically inflated and extended; and the devotion to the truth of the event is the only way to save your soul from this host of temptations that naturally accompany you, down here, during the crossing, up there, on the way back, and in your home on the earth again.

5. A Co-Creative Journey

A preliminary remark is necessary about the nature of the description and translation of spiritual events into ordinary language, before I begin to tell the story of my spiritual journey.

To make the supersensible cooperation between the author and the spiritual worlds comprehensible to ordinary consciousness, I will naturally use our common language, which is based on concepts and images created in the physical world. Because this cooperative research journey took place during the holy days and nights of Christmas 2012, I shaped the story in the images of spiritual conception, pregnancy and birth, to create a modern Christmas Tale. In this respect, I will need the reader's active and creative cooperation, so that a reciprocal translation between us will take place. I will translate the supersensible experiences into physical language, concepts and images and I would ask the reader to spiritualize them again, as far as he or she can do it. I am asking him to do what I do myself with any physically experienced knowledge, which I want to spiritualize and carry to the spiritual worlds. This spiritualization process of the various contents of earthly consciousness, which include all the physical creations and expressions of Rudolf Steiner, not only his spoken and written communications of spiritual knowledge, is the source of the forces necessary to accomplish the opposite task in the spiritual world: to translate the spiritual to the physical and communicate the supersensible experiences in earthly language and images. It is the same cognitive force, working with equal strength in both directions: in the spiritualization of the contents of ordinary cognition and the despiritualization of supersensible cognition.

Therefore, I, for my part, must despiritualize and translate the purely spiritual events, experienced in inspired (immanently thoughtful), and intuited (substantial, being-full), imaginations, into ordinary human thinking, representations and words. And I would ask the reader to accomplish the counter-move: to spiritualize in his or her own soul and consciousness my despiritualizations. For example, I must naturally refer to my spiritual colleagues and teachers as individual beings, and I must use ordinary concepts, expressions, and words like 'individual beings', taken from our daily language in the physical world, in which, naturally, all beings take on physical-bodily form and appearance. This may lead, naturally, to great misunderstandings and confusions regarding the modern communication of spiritual knowledge.

Our modern language is adapted to external physical reality more than in any language in previous times in history. Of course, one could resign and say: since it is altogether impossible to communicate the real spiritual events in ordinary representations and language, and since each such communication means an essential downgrading of the spiritual reality referred to, I prefer to abstain from any communication. Such a purist approach, which is perfectly understandable, is nevertheless unproductive. And the reason is that the spiritual essence and substance transmitted through ordinary communication must not only die in physical expression; it can also transfer some of its deeper vitality to the human soul and heart forces, while it must die in the intellectual forces. The death of the spirit in the dead letter can become a creative act, which does not have to stay buried in its grave. But this depends entirely on what we do, on the receiving end of spiritual creations and knowledge! I cannot prevent it from dying in my ordinary intellect, but it must not end there; I can resurrect it to new life, in my deeper heart and life forces, provided I am willing to greatly awaken and activate all the force and faculties of my soul. It is precisely here that the reader, the one that accepts the gift and sacrifice of the higher worlds, must play his redeeming part. When I am on the receiving end, I must say to myself: I receive the gift of the spiritual worlds from the spiritual scientist in a form that has already been downgraded to adapt it to my ordinary intelligence and language. The spirit lowered itself already a great deal so that I would be able to grasp it in my earthly, common modern intellect; it has died for my evolution's sake. But the essential spirit force, if received not only into the egotistical intellect, emotions and desires, but taken into the deepest heart forces, feelings and deeper will impulses, can awaken in my soul new worlds, and kindle in my heart the fire of faith, love and hope. I feel that while I take in the substance of spiritual communications into my heart and feelings and above all into my active, creative will, and not only into my intellect, excited emotions and desire for knowledge, new forces are awakened in me.

Therefore, I will answer the spirit message and sacrifice, by marshalling my living forces that slumber in the depths of my soul, and resurrect the dead thought forms, representations and words, through which the spiritual gift was delivered. If we truly become conscious of this, we can overcome the purist avoidance of expressing spiritual experiences in ordinary thinking and language. But we will also overcome the other pitfall: to take the spiritual knowledge communicated in physical concepts and representations, assimilate, store, and misuse them in our ordinary waking consciousness. There they will be put to repeated deaths, becoming the plaything of my egotistical speculations, fantasies and undisciplined thinking, feelings and will.

One can say, therefore, that the spiritual scientist and teacher is himself first and foremost an ardent student, and this means that 'teacher' and 'student' are relative and interchangeable terms, and that each must consciously include the other. The spiritual scientist, who conscientiously follows the modern path created by Rudolf Steiner, the founder and pioneer of this wholly new field of human knowledge, must learn to no longer expect a fully formed spiritual revelation to flow down to him, bestowed from above and outside, as was customary and beneficial in ancient times. He must instead learn to actively and creatively raise himself upward towards the spirit and not expect the spirit to be given ready made to him in great and powerful imaginations; he must learn to work on his individual research from below upward or from within outward, until he comes up with a real, pregnant spiritualized problem. He must learn to actively create his or her living concepts and imaginations, and to communicate them to the beings of his colleagues and teachers that stand far above him; he must wait to see if they will take his creations, affirmatively, into themselves and work with them further in the spiritual worlds. In this way, the spiritual scientist, as a pupil of Michael and his collegium, learns the modern art of spiritualizing and transforming human creative thoughts, knowledge, and artistic and social creations, through a co-creative dialogue with the spiritual world. Then — and only then — does the spiritual world come towards you, if you are freely active and creative according to *their* perception and judgement. You will naturally not accord to the imaginations you create real final objective value, but will await until they will be gradually saturated, inspired and intuited from the spiritual world, and will gradually return to you, becoming by degrees—never in any absolute sense—more objective, that is, they will more truly express the real spiritual events, beings, and processes that you want to express. And then again, in your turn, you will look down to ordinary cognition, and will have to de-spiritualize the real spiritual imaginations and adapt them to the ordinary intelligence, language and consciousness of present-day humanity.

This is the reason why the reader is invited to actively co-create with the spiritual researcher, and spiritualize through his own forces the given concepts and representations offered to him. To be awake consciously to this requirement for an active, reciprocal, translation and adaptation between the spiritual investigator and his readers, is of utmost importance in our age. It is unfortunately very common that students of anthroposophy are unaware of the fundamental fact that they receive these golden treasures from the spiritual world to be their loyal custodians and gardeners, as Jesus described it archetypically in his parable about the talents.[*] The treasures should not be wasted and thrown away to the winds in luciferic self-enjoyment, nor conserved in ahrimanic dogmatism, but should be invested in conservative creativity, or creative conservatism, because we will become aware of the secret behind this seeming contradiction. Because we can learn how to draw freely and creatively from the original spiritual source from which the gift was itself created, we can increase its value as the result of free, individualized creation, and return the spiritual capital with thousand-fold interest to its mother source. True spiritual knowledge is given as a living seed, not as finished divine revelation or a dead mental corpse, and this living seed, if properly tended to, in an active,

---

[*] Mathew 25: 14–30.

creative manner, will be properly spiritualized, and given up again to enhance and enrich the source and not our personal vanity.

I would therefore ask my reader to consciously challenge herself: don't take my ordinary language literally and naively, but rather, consciously work to translate my expressions to your most lively experience of their spiritual meaning. Strive to reverse my conscious reversal, try to spiritualize your appropriation of my already stark de-spiritualized translation, and constantly attempt to re-spiritualize your own thinking, feeling and will forces, to make them transparent to the original imaginative and spiritual meanings entrusted to you.

To the extent that this is possible, then, I will describe below some aspects of the supersensible phase of the spiritual becoming process of my book, *Cognitive Yoga*.

* * *

Once the invitation for the spiritual consultation has been received, I undertake all the preparations necessary before one embarks on an exciting and unpredictable journey. (I must, of course, carefully pack my soul-spiritual suitcase, making sure I take with me the necessary spiritual garments, cleansing methods, living waters and energy snacks for the way. However, the actual soul preparations that I make to enter the portal and cross the threshold in a humble and worthy way cannot really be communicated, because they belong to the most intimate personal soul experiences.)

And then past the portal, the power of Imagination awakens fully and lights up. It begins to illuminate a path, and I know that the path is kindly opening itself, in response to the activation of my *seeing*; imaginative consciousness is an active force of doing in this new world. The force of this seeing gradually expands my new visible world, by shedding its light upon the area that I can consciously perceive. There, in this lighted clearing, I am very cordially greeted by a group of spiritual beings, some of them are known to me from previous collaborative tasks, but some are new, and after some jovial welcoming greetings and ceremonial rites of passage, I am most kindly invited to join them on a special mission. I am told (or rather this is how I understand it to begin with) that we are going on a journey to discover and climb to the top of a very special mountain. The journey itself is a highly stimulating and wonderful experience as the fellowship accomplishes many fascinating explorations and investigations of the spiritual ecosystem through which we pass, supervised by members of the team who seem to command infinite knowledge of the spiritual mysteries of nature and cosmos. Eventually we come to a stop, and when I wonder why, as there was no mountain in sight, one of my comrades tells me, in a kind of matter-of-fact tone: here we are going to *create* the mountain. (Now I begin to realize that it was my misunderstanding all along, while everybody else was obviously perfectly aware of this, that we were not going to find a mountain, but rather to create one.) We are therefore getting ready to camp at this location, and to begin with, some rituals are performed, with that rare combination of solemnity during the ceremonies and exuberantly joyful and creative fun immediately thereafter, which seems to make up the daily rhythm and pulse of these illustrious beings. I realize eventually that these rituals are performed to acclimatize ourselves to the spiritual forces of the spiritual land and the spiritual cosmic surroundings, which, unfortunately, I cannot recall in precise outlines, because my consciousness was not sharp enough to grasp and comprehend its real nature in real time, and hence I cannot recall them in exact detail when I am back in my ordinary consciousness on the earth. (This is something that I would wish to be able to do better, on future occasions, as I am very interested in the spiritual nature and becoming of spiritual cosmic climate, weather, and the planetary and starry forces active through the universe.) After all these wonderful events have been commenced, we are told that the mountain creation work can begin.

The creation process of the mountain is revealed as something wholly different from everything I have experienced before in previous research consultations. It turns out that all my companions are magically creative beings, and each one of them has a matchless, utterly individual, way of procuring the needed materials for the work of construction. They all possess an awe-inspiring capacity: each one of them brings forth, in a rather mysterious way, out of his own being, precious metals, gems, and other remarkable stones, most of which I haven't seen on the earth. And they build this mountain from these precious metals, gems and stones. Now I know that I am expected to join the work, which, somewhat awkwardly, I believe that I can also do. In a rather naive way—that will be embarrassingly disclosed soon enough—I feel that I can also bring forth my building materials out of myself, as I have a distinct, bodily sensation, that my body harbours them and really desires to give them birth. And indeed, in no time at all, I have my hands full of some stuff that I cannot recognize right away. Nevertheless, I begin to mould it and insert it into the mountain that meanwhile is becoming a spectacular creation to behold. But then, rather startlingly, I first experience, and then actually *see* (and unfortunately also smell, touch, taste and so on), that what I have in my hands, what I am adding to all these wonderful precious metals, gems and stones, appears to be only murky mud! I feel greatly exposed and self-conscious, naturally, realizing that I am so utterly unworthy of truly helping this heavenly job, and that I am really ruining the great work with my messy contributions.

But then, what happens next is even more astounding. I see that some of the divine master-builders take my muddy stuff and matter of factly transform it into the most beautiful and pure crystalline formations. And they all kindly and merrily encourage me to continue to supply them with more mud, and truly, my body and hands happen to be willing to generously fulfil their request, which allows them to show me in detail and expertise how they transform it to something far better, far more beautiful than I could ever imagine.

After what seemed (by our earthly time standards) to be a very long, labourious and creative day, we are summoned to gather around our creation, and what takes place now can be compared only to a spiritual scientific study session, in which the master-builders describe with great expertise, joy and satisfaction the real purpose of their joint creation. (I can only mention here the smallest part of this spiritual master-class.) To put it in very simplistic earthly terms, this instruction has the effect on my cognitive forces that I begin to see and comprehend what was totally veiled from me before: that the mountain is, precisely speaking, no mountain at all but a beautifully and harmoniously constructed, archetypal, cosmic spiritual *being*, which a future spiritual epoch will need, because it will be its task to incarnate and embody this cosmic being in an appropriate spiritual body on the earth. And indeed, only now it starts to dawn on me, in what sense this spiritual expedition and project relates to my research problem, described above. Now I begin to see the concrete connections between my research problem and this demonstration of great spiritual work, and why I could participate in this profound mystery, and to even see in what sense the results of my most humble research can offer a contribution to this sublime future cosmic-human project.

Now the headmaster of the illustrious company, who kept rather quiet until then (in the limited compass of my spiritual awareness, I could before only sense his presence and activities in the background, where he was coordinating our efforts with hardly visible higher and wider circles and beings), stepped forward, and began to speak. I could recognize him now for the first time, and connect this imaginative appearance with the being of the spiritual teacher, whom I know on the earth through his intimate soul-spiritual companionship. What made this identification possible, was not his imaginative form of appearance (which was totally different from his physical form in his last earthly lives), but the special *tone* of his speech, which has that unmistakable quality, that resounds the same in all worlds. I felt immediately that he directs his words to the centre of my heart. And while he was speaking, I was wholly taken over by the power, beauty and infinite grace of the love forces that poured forth through his words. I felt that his speech had such a magical moral power to it, that it is capable not only to move existing mountains and create new ones, but also to create whole new universes. And yet it was infinitely gentle and human, soft spoken and liberating, at the same time. I was utterly awe stricken by this event, about which I can say the very least, though it seemed to continue for an immensely long and blessed, blissful, eternity. And this is a fundamental spiritual condition, that all honest and serious students of spiritual science must be aware of: I could only grasp what he has spoken, to the extent that his teaching on the earth, has borne true fruit in my soul, and that this fruit now becomes an organ of spiritual comprehension. In truth, I can only see and comprehend anything in the spiritual world, in its true being, to the extent that I have first assimilated and spiritualized it thoroughly on the earth, through the study of what the teacher himself communicated from his experiences. And therefore, I can only translate his cosmic-heart words into earthly human words, concepts and images, to the extent that I have learned to embody and spiritualize his teachings and experience his spiritual being through this work in my physical life. This is also the only way I can spiritually activate them, renew them again, and *remember* them now in earthly cognition, and become *mindful* of them, and eventually *see* them again here and now: by repeatedly and intensively spiritualizing his spiritual scientific teachings in my individual cognition and life on the earth. This earthly activity is what becomes a living organ of spiritual seeing in the supersensible worlds, and it alone can reawaken the living echo of this seeing in ordinary earthly consciousness. The cognitive, creative, and free spiritual activity—which he called, in his most beloved book, *The Philosophy of Freedom*, 'love in its spiritual form', that he actualized himself and taught on the earth, is ultimately—for us humans in this cosmic age—the only true universal language and translator, between all worlds and all beings, between all stages and states of consciousness, from the lowest to the very highest.

Now his Word stream flowed as he spoke through my whole being into my heart, and downward through me, as it were, and as it did so, it made the earth appear, which wasn't visible in the limited compass of my conscious spiritual awareness before. His love-filled words, dedicated for the salvation of earth and humanity, really made the earth appear below us as a heavenly chalice, shimmering and glowing with the most sublime auric colours. He said (we must imagine that this speech is an Imaginative flow of world-creating Imaginations, and every Imagination is in itself like a whole universe of creative cosmic becoming, while each word and sentence is bringing forth, gathering, shaping and moulding the spiritual forms, substances and realities about which he speaks): 'When I was last incarnated on the earth in a physical human body, before the great catastrophe that divided human evolution into two wholly distinct parts, I tried to find human hearts, to plant this seed in them, as a Foundation Stone made of the quintessence of freedom and love, in which I concentrated all the harvest of my previous earthly life and labour. This spiritualized essence had many names through history. It was called the Holy Grail, or heavenly Jerusalem, which is another name also for the next future Jupiter embodiment of the earth. But this Foundation Stone, is really the true, divine being of the human being. And for the first time in the course of human evolution, *this* archetypal human being was born on earth in the Christmas Foundation Conference of 1923–4. As I said back then on the earth, before my death, the Foundation Stone is the new cosmic, spiritually free and creative human being, the "individual human being active and creative inside the human-cosmic being", working in full consciousness with his fellow humans, nature, cosmos and hierarchies. This cosmic threefold, spiritual-soul and bodily human being, is the firstborn, *purely human,* creation and embodiment of the being of Anthroposophia, born from the free individuation of the union of Christ's "I" impulse and the eternal cosmic Sophia. This is my mission through the coming cosmic age, to help each human being to give birth, nourish, foster and grow his and her true self as the creation of free humanity in the age of the consciousness soul. This new born cosmic human being experienced its fire baptism and initiation in the mysteries of evil during the 12 years, 1933–1945. There it participated actively in the great deeds of sacrifice that took place in the etheric world and continue also today.* Since then it is the Foundation Stone of the mysteries of the Michaelic age: the mysteries of the new humanity and the sun-becoming of the earth through humanity. It is fashioned by means of the purely human forces of freedom and loving sacrifice, and we must now, in the twenty-first century, find people that will be able to individualize it and incarnate it in its new form on the earth.'

After he completed his cosmic yet entirely human speech, I could, for the first time, begin to surmise, still vaguely, the deeper meaning of my research problem and its solution. I could see how my clumsy and imperfect work on the earth is contributing to the human and cosmic great work of creating the burgeoning archetype of new earthly-cosmic human being, which is the project all the masters of humanity prepared since immemorial times, and that through Rudolf Steiner found its first fully human incarnation. The new fully individualized and self-conscious cosmic human being is also the nucleus of the new, humanly created, resurrection body of humanity and the earth.

When this sacred intimation was dawning in my soul I could see down below on the spiritual earth, a cosmic Imagination of the Foundation Stone as the creation of the new cosmic human being. It appeared as coming to incarnation, birth, and development, through the Imagination of the Christ Impulse in the aura of the whole earth. His speech now took the form of demonstrating, showing how the being of the new human being, Anthroposophia, emerges from the shining crystalline formation, the golden star, that he des-

---

*In the book, *The Spiritual Event of the Twentieth Century: The Occult Significance of the 12 years, 1933–1945, in the Light of Spiritual Science; an Imagination,* I tried to put in words some aspects of this postmortem biography of Rudolf Steiner and the being of Anthroposophia.

cribed only once, in a lecture given in 1918 in Berlin. This Imagination that for decades was an essential part of my meditations, was now entirely transformed, and I became aware that the Foundation Stone—the new cosmic human being—born on the earth in the Christmas Foundation Conference, is a direct offspring of the Mystery of Golgotha.

I will quote this passage here because it alone can present the meaning of what was experienced above:

> When a dead person in our present era observes certain places, then from the place which here on Earth is known as Palestine, as Jerusalem, something with a golden form, a golden crystal form, is to be seen in the middle of the bluish-mauve colour and this becomes animated. That is the Jerusalem as seen from the spirit! This it is which also in the Apocalypse figures as the heavenly Jerusalem. These are not 'thought-out' things, they are things which can be observed, seen spiritually. The Mystery of Golgotha appeared like what physical observation perceives when the astronomer directs his telescope to space and beholds something which fills him with wonder, like, for example the flashing-up of new stars. Seen spiritually, from the Universe, the Event of Golgotha was the flashing-up of a star of gold in the blue aura of the Eastern half of the Earth. Try to think with someone who has passed over, of the crystal form of the heavenly Jerusalem building itself up into golden splendour in the bluish-violet aura of the Earth. Uncover that, and that will bring you near to him; for that is something which belongs to the realm of the Imaginations into which the dying person enters at death: 'Out of God we are born, and in Christ we die'.*

As this Imagination was shown, I could now *see* the birth of the free spiritual being of humanity since last century, as an offspring of many bigger and smaller sacred events in the whole spiritual evolution of humanity since the most

---
*Lecture of 1 April 1918, in GA 181.

primeval ages to the far distant future times. But above all, three dramatic cosmic-earthly breakthroughs, three major recent spiritual events stood out, and the third of them, the great cosmic event of the beginning of the twentieth century, was demonstrated to be their offspring. First, it was seen in the lightning and thunder of Mount Sinai, through the eternal flames of the Burning Bush, in which, in the fiery letters of the sacred script, God's true name, dwelling in Christ, could be expressed in the earthly world: *Eheje Asher Eheje*, I AM that I AM; secondly, it was seen as the central event of earthly evolution as a whole, in the physically incarnating Christ, the fulfillment of the meaning of the earth and humanity, conceived in Jesus in the baptism in Jordan, and born as the sun spirit of the earth in the Mystery of Golgotha; and third, the first purely human offspring of this event, was born as a creation of humanity's cosmic becoming. This world-changing event took place in the above referred to Christmas Foundation Conference of 1923-4, during which the new cosmic human being was born, whose essence was expressed in the Foundation Stone Meditation. Again, I have been living and meditating this sacred event for decades, and I experienced its central significance to human evolution, from ever deeper points of view. But now I could *see* its significance in a wholly new, objective, way. I could truly grasp for the first time Rudolf Steiner's specific new mission among the great teachers of humanity. Eternally born through the Christ's deeds in Sinai, Jordan and Jerusalem, moving from the East to Israel, to incarnate in the middle of the earth, it moved further westward, and was individualized, conceived and born anew as a fully free human deed and being, through Rudolf Steiner, in the middle of Europe, in order to find refuge again in the middle of the earth, in the holy land, after the devastating, world-shattering and changing apocalypse of the twentieth century. There, in the middle of the earth, the broken bridge could be forged again between the physical world and the spiritual world, between earthly and heavenly Jerusalem. And I could experience, with my whole being, that it is this being that is now asking to be multiplied and born in each single human being, in our active and creative free cognition and loving social life on the earth, wherever we work, aspire and dedicate ourselves to our true future human becoming.

And now, as if waiting for the completion of my inner realization, the teacher signalled all to gather around this Imagination of the crystalline, golden cosmic star, glowing and shimmering with all the bountiful colours of the precious metals, gems and stones growing with it. And now as all the beings, from near and afar, united themselves together, each and all in perfect harmony and synergy, and painted together, speaking, dancing, singing, as a mighty choir, in the astral light, a sublime Imagination in the blue-purple aura of the earth appeared; and with each word-gesture, musical composition, formative dance cycle, and cosmic painting and movement, I could see how the golden star of heavenly Jerusalem flares up, with ever stronger force of life and radiance. I realized that they are speaking, sculpting, performing, dancing, and painting the imagination of the future, empowering and perfecting the future spiritualized cosmic human being, humanity and the earth; and that they wish to inspire me and all humans for all future ages to come, that we shall have faith in ourselves and in our humble but irreplaceable cosmic contribution. They wish to convey that in our age mortal humans like us must grow and have the courage to participate in this great work—through many small and great deeds of love and sacrifice—in individualizing this seed of spirit, soul and bodily resurrection and new human and earth formation. And I felt warmly encouraged to actualize this truth, and carry it with me back to the earth, as a golden, potent spiritual-soul bodily seed, as an earnest, sacred and festive, Christmas nativity event. I felt impregnated and fructified by the returning, confirmed, substantiated, and infinitely enhanced and spiritualized essence of my research, coming back to me, as a new creative power. I felt now that with its help, I may venture once more to try and cross the lower bodily threshold with renewed forces, overcome the dead and hardened soul and body shells, encasements and sedimentations, that blocked my way before; that now I may be able to find and awaken, stimulate and activate, the body's pure, original, virgin forces of humanity, and unite them with Christ's presently active, living etheric body; and that I would be supported in my renewed efforts to achieve this goal by means of the Michaelic forces of the present Michaelic age, immortalized through Rudolf Steiner's eternally productive life in us.

6. The Author is Pregnant

During the time of pregnancy, between the spiritual conception and physical birth, my whole soul life undergoes a profound, if imperceptible and subtle, metamorphosis. I feel that my inner life, thoughts, feelings, and all my daily experiences, are linked to the research project in such a way that a parallel and interrelated development is taking place in my own soul and in the spiritual world. I am fully conscious that my mothering soul womb is a 'shared womb', because the developing spiritual research project is just as much outside my soul, in the external spiritual world, as it is within it (this is also the case in human physical pregnancy, and indeed some mothers are aware of this). I am aware that this developing being is living, moving and kicking, both in my inner life as well as in the spiritual world, where it is carried and protected by a community of creative beings, my above-mentioned colleagues, mentors and partners. The two processes, in my own soul and in the spiritual world, are mutually interactive and supportive. For example, it is apparent that each one of them considers the research project to be his and her own baby as well, and, what is more, they all experience themselves together, as a community, to be the mothering and fathering guardians and benefactors of its earthly becoming.

This is a very special time for me, because I must remain attentive to what this spiritual being growing in my soul needs for its becoming. I ask myself daily about the best ways to support its healthy development. I am concerned with the spiritual baby's nourishment and development very much like a mother who is conscious of how she nourishes the baby developing in her womb with her thoughts, feelings and what she eats and drinks. However, during the general time of pregnancy, with its established and long-term rhythms, other times intervene, in which the baby project undergoes more pronounced transformations, that demand special nourishment and care.

I feel, at certain times, an inner push or impulse, to give my regular spiritual work a more definite intensity and consistency. I am aware that this impulse originates from the being of the work itself and not only from my own inner life. When I experience this impulse I already know from previous experiences that something of significance is being prepared. I know, to put it rather simply, that the spiritual baby — and with it the beings that carry and support it in the spiritual world — is asking for some specific nourishment that it needs in this specific stage of growth and metamorphosis, in order go through a definite and timely process of development.

Then in my spiritual experience it often happens — in critical stages of the pregnancy of the research this becomes especially noticeable — that I am invited again to participate in its spiritual becoming process in the spiritual world, only now I stay down here, as it were, in my body, and must find a way to collaborate and coordinate its embryonic becoming and metamorphosis with my partners from here. Again, such invitations are experienced as a gift and grace, because one becomes conscious that one's thoughts, feelings and experiences, originating in one's own inner soul life, are called for, and can be infinitely enhanced and perfected by the spiritual world and become objective world formative forces.

Through the years, I have learned to bring to full consciousness some of these interactive processes while continuing my regular life in the physical body. Then I experience that not only does the spiritual world take up and transform the materials and processes that I prepared for the research's embryonic development, but that also my very human being is taken up and used for the better. (During this process, I also experience how infinitely distant I am from my Higher Self that my colleagues consider—so generously and gracefully—as a worthy partner in their creative work. However, thanks to their infinitely positive and loving respect for all life, including my own, I don't experience this comparison as reproach or judgement, but rather as a kind empowerment and stimulation to continue and work on myself and progress by means of my own personal efforts.)

Let me offer a concrete example of how this nourishment process is brought about.

As I said above, at certain moments in the embryonic development of the research, I feel prompted to take special measures, and provide the growing baby with especially vital spiritual nourishment. In these times, I take special measures to awaken in my heart intimations, feelings, moods, dispositions related to the above described spiritual co-creative journey, to let it silently echo and reverberate in my soul. This is not done to *repeat* the original supersensible experience, but to awaken the deeper soul forces that carry its echoes in the otherwise unconscious regions of the soul. When I succeed in this, and my soul is warmly awake to these feelings and intimations, I feel I can prepare myself to participate more consciously in the creative process that is taking place in my soul and in the spiritual worlds, and their mutual interactions. For this purpose, I have developed the following meditation.

The relationships between what takes place in the soul of the spiritual scientist and his colleagues in the spiritual worlds after conception, can be likened to a reversal of the physical relationships between the flowering plant and the forces of the sun. Physically speaking, in the sun sphere we have the source of the light and warmth forces, towards which the etheric and physical bodies of the plant are growing and evolving on the earth. The spiritual archetype, the *Urpflanze*, of the whole plant kingdom, lives and weaves between the sun sphere above and the middle of the earth below, and on the earth each single plant species and each single individual plant embodies one variant of it, nourished and supported by the forces of the earth, water, and air from below and the light and warmth from the sun. The sun appears in this respect to be the universal mother source and the earth as the father force, individuating and differentiating, expressing the cosmic sun archetype through multitudes of single plants, each existing and thriving as a separate organism in time and space. Indeed, this was also the human situation in the past when human personalities on the earth were like branches of the group souls, that contained also the universal higher self of humanity, that lived in the sun sphere. But since the Mystery of Golgotha this relation has been essentially reversed, though, naturally, it takes thousands of years to show itself in the lives of self-conscious human beings. The universal, archetypal being of humanity, its Idea, the I AM, dramatically transferred the centre of His being and becoming from the sun to the earth and the depths of the human soul. This means that the spiritual source of true human creations, can be found in the embodied, active and creative forces of any self-spiritualizing and self-actualizing soul. After 2000 years, in the age of the Consciousness or Spiritual Soul, this begins to be possible to all human beings. This is the reason why spiritual science can be given to humanity for the first time in this age, because it works and creates consciously with these divine forces on the earth. If my work is truly rooted in the sun spirit that became the spirit of the earth, that lives and weaves now down here, on the earth, I will look in vain to find the universal spiritual source of my creation in the spiritual world above, because it lives and weaves right here, in the depths of my own being. A magnificent, all-transforming cosmic event has taken place, and from now on, the being and becoming of the individual human being is the only place in which the immanent essence of the universal, archetypal source can be found. The individual is becoming the universal, since the universal I AM is already individualized, potentially, in every personality. And each human being can, from this age onward, freely choose to actualize and develop this individual potential. The self-conscious human individuality is not any longer a branch of a group being, or a copy of a collective spiritual archetype; through Christ's deed of infinite sacrifice, exchanging the sun for the earth as his new cosmic abode, the higher self and archetype of each human being has become an incarnated, individualized, singularity. Now the human spirit in its self-conscious and creative spiritual activity can become—in physical life between birth and death—a source of spiritual creation, that previously could only be found in the higher worlds. And as previously the cosmic archetype expressed itself in so many individuals and species on the earth, today the reverse is as true. When the human soul and spirit, living in its bodies, freely activates and actualizes itself spiritually, in full self-consciousness, it becomes an earthly-sun creative source, that radiates its creative expressions from the earth below to the spiritual worlds above; it expresses itself in the spiritual worlds through its creative deeds on the earth, which the beings of the spiritual worlds can harvest and work with further. They can develop my new creations and multiply them in infinite individual variations, disseminated and shared with all the beings of the universe as fresh, life-giving nourishment, to enhance their evolution.

This is, therefore, my permanent meditation during this spiritual-soul pregnancy: I picture the cosmic sun being radiating from below through the whole earth, as the spirit of the earth, working in the earth under my feet, through my body, filling the whole light-giving atmosphere, as the archetypal *earthly* spiritual source. I picture it as an earthly-sun being, undulating rhythmically in the atmosphere and through my breathing, flowing with the circulation of the blood through my whole body, becoming in the head a generative force of spiritual cognition. This meditation becomes the vital, nourishing, link with both the supersensible experience described above, which is the heart and soul of my research problem and its solution, and with the presently active and supporting colleagues in the spiritual world. They, in turn respond with a greater influx of parenting support, inspiration and guidance. This meditation strengthens me and my research baby and supplies it with continuous stream of fresh and highly nourishing life forces, which the growing embryo must receive in decisive stages of metamorphosis and growth.

As the research pregnancy develops, I dedicate a portion of my daily meditations and experiences to this process, and let its results flow upward to my colleagues. I don't try to specify and intentionally direct the way my work should be used by my colleagues in the higher worlds. I know perfectly well that they have their far wiser ways! So, I let them decide how, where and when the fruits of my inner work should nourish the research embryo. The above described meditation has proved itself fruitful, in creating this reciprocal exchange, as a secure and pure channel of cooperation and collaborative work, during the research's embryonic development.

7. A Book is Born

Near the final stages of the soul-spiritual pregnancy, I usually feel the growing need to sketch some things out, either drawing them or writing them down in short sentences in my notebook. Sometimes I post a short passage about my ongoing research on Facebook or on my blog, and I often feel the impulse to say a word or two about it in my lectures. This allows me to test the waters both inside me and outside me in the real world.

I have discovered that this is an organic and important part of the ripening process. These preliminary physical expressions constitute an essential threefold feedback loop between the physical world, my soul that harbours the being of the research, and the spiritual world that continues to nourish it from its own side. This feedback loop is also rhythmic, like all the previous processes, because rhythm is life, and all spiritual work and research is alive. But then a crucial change comes and I begin to feel that the work is kindly requesting — and sometimes also pushing! — to be born. Its promptings are obviously not as acute as what the physical mother experiences, but on the soul and spirit level, it can take on unmistakable forms. It is a markedly bodily sensation, especially between head, heart, and hands, which says: I must be expressed! You must write me down! Or talk, paint, dance, initiate a social action! It is this sensation of bodily-soul pressure that counts most and will eventually decide the moment of starting the actual intensive physical-external expression. In this way, I know for sure that it is not coming from my own personal wishes or desires, say, to finally publish, move on, or attract external attention. It is as objective as physical birth pangs.

When the time of birth arrives, it must be understood that the time needed for the 'travails of birth' is as much a part of the creative process as any other.

Now, what happens next is, again, a result of repeated experience. When the prompting becomes, so to say, unbearable, and I finally decide to begin to write the book down, something happens that is always surprising. Before, during pregnancy, I actively recreated in my soul the moods and feelings of the original supersensible experience, and now the result of this recreation condenses itself. It is transformed into a new force that penetrates even deeper, into the body itself. I feel that it brings down and embodies the solution to my research problem, transformed into a process which awakens and activates all the deeper levels of my physically incarnated being. It is not taking me up to itself, to the purely supersensible spiritual world, as the original experience did, nor is it part of the soul experiences I had during pregnancy. It works like a force that flows all the way down into my physical body. It is a rather formless force or impulse, awakening the will forces in the body. The embodied moods, reminiscences and echoes of the original imaginative formative forces, will light up consciously gradually later, from the other side, as it were, streaming from the body to the head; then they will energize and vitalize the devitalized stream of thoughts and language formation, while I am already engaged in physical writing. But at this juncture it first transforms and concentrates the imaginative elements and forces into an impulse of will, activity and dynamic energy. When I was writing *Cognitive Yoga*, I experienced how these concentrated formative forces of the original supersensible experience helped me when I was struggling to express it in a book form.

This applies to the *will force*, that to begin with, flows into the bodies from the transformed supersensible experience. But concerning the *content* of the experience, that one will communicate eventually in thinking and language, the following must be borne in mind.

It must be emphasized that fully conscious supersensible experiences, that result from real spiritual scientific work, cannot be remembered as psychic and clairvoyant visions. The clairvoyant received his imaginations as a given fact, and forms his representations of them in the same way as we perceive our physical environment with our senses and form representations of what we see, hear, touch and smell. As described above, in spiritual scientific work, nothing is simply given; all the stages of the work are done in full consciousness. The content of a fully conscious imaginative perception is not given, but must be actively produced and then corrected and augmented by the spiritual worlds. It is the result of an active, creative and free collaboration. Memory as we know is based on the fact that we receive our sense impressions passively into our bodies and minds. This applies to physical sense perceptions as well as to visionary experiences, and it doesn't exist in fully conscious supersensible cognition. We must say, therefore, that all the stages of spiritual, imaginative cognition, from perception to conception and expression, must be done in full consciousness. The preparation is a creative conscious process; the supersensible experience is an active co-production with the beings of the spiritual worlds, and therefore also its transformation process to physical expression is a fully conscious creative work. It is fully human, that is, the whole human soul participates, in a conscious, active, manner, in this spiritual co-production, from beginning to end. Therefore, it is not possible to 'remember' it in the ordinary, passive, unconscious way that our memory operates on the earth.

How is it then at all possible to communicate spiritual knowledge in earthly thoughts, representations and words? This is one of the deepest mysteries of truly modern spiritual cognition. It makes an essential difference between spiritual science and all older spiritual practices, that originated before the full maturity of the consciousness soul. In spiritual science, imaginative cognition is a direct result of the transformation of the consciousness soul, developed by means of a gradual and fully conscious spiritualization of the forces of self-conscious modern cognition. The imaginative experiences will be fully clear, transparent, and inwardly, immanently, thought through. That is, we will not have to 'think about them' with our ordinary thinking to represent, interpret and understand them, because they think and speak about themselves directly in the experience itself. If we now wish to be able to 'remember' these experiences in ordinary consciousness, we must—again in fullest consciousness—transform, devitalize, despiritualize them *consciously*; and only the result of this conscious, highly spiritual despiritualization process can be translated into pure thinking, and from there, by means of the physical brain, be devitalized further until it lights up in us as the content of ordinary representations. Only these conceptual representations can be remembered. This despiritualization must be practised in fullest, most living, cognition, and then it is remembered and can be communicated in ordinary language in the physical world.[*]

This whole process naturally demands some measure of disciplined attention and awareness, and much loving patience. What will ignite the impulse of writing, then, will be

---

[*] I have described this process in detail, from various points of view, in my books, *The New Experience of the Supersensible*, *The Event in Science, History, Philosophy & Art*, and in *Cognitive Yoga*.

the coming together of the two distinct streams that originate in the supersensible experience: the one that flows as a living force into the bodily will forces, and the other that comes from the above described despiritualization of the contents of the supersensible experience. The first stream stimulates the will forces to awaken in the body during the physical writing; the second brings the content into clear thinking. When the first stream has embodied itself sufficiently, it becomes a firing impulse that awakens thinking to new life through the whole body. It begins to gather itself together from the whole body, and stream into the head, heart and hands, and connect them together. Then I experience the emergence of a fresh flow of life forces, that revitalize—but now in and through the body—my consciously devitalized representations, and allow them to stream to my thoughts and fingertips. And only then the real process of physical thinking, wording, writing, begins.

As the writing develops, I must, naturally, experience the usual disturbances, coming from the body and the physical environment. After all, as I think and write, the body continues to serve loyally the gift of physical life, and the soul is still embodied, and continues to feel the ordinary bodily sensations of comfort and discomfort, hunger and thirst, tiredness, pain, etc. And of course, I also continue to be part of everyday life while I am writing: the news, conversations with people, and the ordinary impressions from my environment are all still there! (Let me add that I never felt a need to retreat physically to remote or quiet places in order to write; I can write as well in a crowded coffee shop in the middle of a bustling city, and actually prefer this noise as it stimulates me to create my inner peace and keep it intact.)

In any event, unlike the soul and spiritual experiences, which take place outside the nerves and sense system and their constant physical stimulation, the writing process is exposed to the entire human bodily-soul life. Writing is bodily manual work; it is real physical labour taking place here and now, and the brain and senses, breathing, heartbeats, discomforts of body and moods of the soul continue as usual.

Therefore, each physical expression of spiritual experience and research requires the creation of a suitable procedure and discipline, to help it come through to the physical world. During the writing of the book *Cognitive Yoga*, a substantial part of which is concerned with the etherization of sensory and bodily processes, I had to develop an appropriate inner discipline that allowed me to work in and through the body, while sustaining a conscious state of being periodically disconnected from impressions, sensations and affections from inside and outside. For this purpose, I could use my acquired practice of creating a state of deep stillness, of soul and bodily peace and tranquility, which I use for my spiritual investigations. While usually I apply it to support higher states of consciousness during spiritual explorations, I have learned to modify it and apply it to the body as well; to think, articulate and write, while remaining in the body. The development and sustaining of this force of stillness required some experimentation, and then I had to also create the appropriate cognitive tools to work with it. I can also say that in order to write down the complex and multilevelled research project of *Cognitive Yoga*, I had to embody it in its spiritual bodily essence, while being incarnated and active physically.

From the moment that the birth pangs of the book began, the writing became a vital stream and an uninterrupted, continuous flow. But this process is also a rhythmic one, changing between more spiritually oriented research and the physical writing. This breathing was always essential for keeping the writing connected to the spiritual processes that I was describing. I had to constantly reactivate my cognitive yoga practice and research, on the one hand, and then delve with it back into the writing bodily process on the other, interchangeably. Finally, I could experience, while fully conscious in the physical body and during the physical typing of the thoughts through my fingertips on the keyboard of my laptop, that my body was becoming part of the flow, in which there is only one stream, one life and one activity that pulses and streams and weaves from the spirit to soul and from the soul to the spiritualized processes of the bodies.

The bodily incarnation and birth is the final stage in the creative spiritual process which completes the seasonal cycle, composed of the four spiritual phases of spiritual creativity, described above in the first chapter. It begins with the spiritualization process that leads to the ripening of an unsolvable problem, continues to the purely supersensible experience that addresses it, and is followed by fertilization and conception, pregnancy and birth of the work in the physical world. This breathing rhythm between the physical and spiritual worlds, the mutual fertilization and cooperative conception of the research, become, in its totality, an expression of the Michael impulse in the present age of Michael. This impulse must find a way to transform the spiritual human being in its entirety, penetrating also into the physical body itself. When one works in the above described way, seeking Michael's help in overcoming the lower bodily threshold, one may find the strongest support; one knows that the way to the Christ, both in its etheric revelation and in the depth of the human bodies, can be trodden, through truly active spiritual scientific work.

As my research process confirms, when the human being spiritualizes his earthly consciousness and activity in this manner, he also allows Michael to work back on his being and spiritualize his bodily constitution. The spiritual harvest becomes a new spiritualizing configuration and formation of the human bodies, from their most primordial foundations, working eventually so deeply as to transform the physical body of the future. A new 'Michaelic body' is thus created, based on the Christ-permeated bodies described above. In this manner, an organic, continuous evolution is achieved, between the Christ impulse and the Michael impulse in our present age, in which the etheric Second Coming is taking place:

> These Michael impulses enter even into the forces that are otherwise determined merely by the connections of race and nation... Now the Michaelic Intelligence is on the earth, now it strikes far deeper, it strikes down even into the earthly element of man. For the first time, the Spiritual is preparing to become a spiritualized, body-creating force... Thus, that which is influenced by Michael will appear as an immediate, physically creative, physically formative power.[*]

The greatest fulfilment and joy of this whole conception, pregnancy and delivery, is that I am taking part in a creative unfolding in which the content and structure of what will be later incarnated as a new thought sequence, passage, chapter, or even a single, pregnant word, is being 'worked through' in my very body by the whole cosmos. I experience that my creative inner soul and spiritual process has become in this manner an integral part of an objective spiritual becoming, even in the physical world. I perceive that a small part of this process, albeit fragmented and limited, will eventually find — with God's grace — its incarnation, expression and earthly birth in a body of a physical lecture, human meeting, artistic event or book.

---
[*] Lecture of 3 August 1924, GA 237.

During the intensification of my research during the holy days and nights of 2012, which were later embodied in *Cognitive Yoga: Making Yourself a New Etheric Body and Individuality* (2016), I felt a need to share some of those experiences with my colleagues. This sharing, which has also now been fully born as the younger brother or sister to *Cognitive Yoga* in the form of the book which you are reading, has this goal: to make us aware that we are taking part in this same creative process all the time. This knowledge may heighten our shared consciousness and deepen our feeling of mutual creative, joyful, responsibility, and help us to become conscious co-creators with the creative beings that support and nourish this new and great earthly-human sun work. In this way, we may rightly feel that we are taking part in the realization of the present, second, Michaelic revelation:

> 'The Word becoming flesh is the first Michael revelation; the flesh becoming Spirit must be the second Michael revelation.'[*]

---

[*] GA 194, 22 November 1919.